Spotlight on
ANCIENT CIVILIZATIONS
GREECE

# Ancient Greek
# GEOGRAPHY

Henry Bensinger

Published in 2014 by The Rosen Publishing Group, Inc.
29 East 21st Street, New York, NY 10010

First Edition

Editor: Joanne Randolph
Book Design: Kate Vlachos

Photo Credits: Cover Tuul/Robert Harding World Imagery/Getty Images; p. 4 Calek/Shutterstock.com; p. 5 Duncan Walker/E+/Getty Images; p. 7 Panoramic Images/Getty Images; pp. 8, 9, 12, 16 DEA/G. Dagli Orti/De Agostini/Getty Images; p. 10 Lenar Musin/Shutterstock.com; p. 11 © iStockphoto.com/Adrian Assalve; p. 13 Vartanov Anatoly/Shutterstock.com; p. 14 Universal Images Group/Getty Images; p. 15 stefanel/Shutterstock.com; p. 17 Nomad_Soul/Shutterstock.com; p. 18 DEA/G. Nimatallah/De Agostini/Getty Images; p. 19 bopra77/Shutterstock.com; p. 20 iStockphoto/Thinkstock; p. 21 Panos Karas/Shutterstock.com; p. 22 Jean-Pierre Lescourret/Lonely Planet Images/Getty Images.

Library of Congress Cataloging-in-Publication Data

Bensinger, Henry.
  Ancient Greek geography / by Henry Bensinger. — First Edition.
     p. cm. — (Spotlight on ancient civilizations. Greece)
  Includes index.
  ISBN 978-1-4777-0773-9 (library binding) — ISBN 978-1-4777-0879-8 (pbk.) — ISBN 978-1-4777-0880-4 (6-pack)
  1. Greece—Civilization—To 146 B.C.—Juvenile literature. 2. Greece—Geography—Juvenile literature. 3. Natural resources—Greece—History—To 1500—Juvenile literature. I. Title.
  DF78.B394 2014
  913.8—dc23
                                        2013000749

Manufactured in the United States of America

CPSIA Compliance Information: Batch #S13PK2: For Further Information contact Rosen Publishing, New York, New York at 1-800-237-9932

# CONTENTS

# The Geography of Ancient Greece

Greece is a **peninsula** and a group of islands in the Mediterranean Sea. It has a rugged and rocky landscape. In fact, nearly 80 percent of Greece is covered in mountains. This made it a hard place

This is the rocky coast of the Greek island of Cephalonia. This mountainous island has a lot of earthquakes. The people of ancient Greece likely grew olive trees and raised goats here.

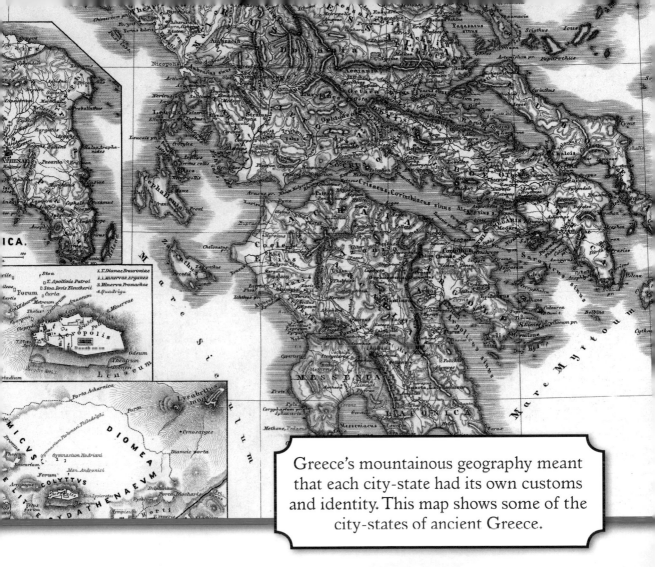

Greece's mountainous geography meant that each city-state had its own customs and identity. This map shows some of the city-states of ancient Greece.

to live for the people of ancient Greece. Most people in ancient Greece were farmers. Yet there was not that much farmable land.

However, there were other **natural resources** available to the ancient Greeks. The rocky land had many **mineral deposits**. The nearby sea meant fish were also a plentiful resource.

# Climate

The **climate** of ancient Greece depended on the area. The three main areas were the coast, the mountains, and the lowlands. The areas on the coast and in the lowlands had long, dry summers. Some areas were very hot in the summer, but other areas stayed mild due to coastal breezes. The winters were generally short and wet.

Mountainous areas in ancient Greece were much colder than the coasts and lowland areas. Winters were snowy. This snow melted in the summer and supplied Greece's rivers and streams with water. It also allowed **pastures** to grow in the mountains.

Even today, mountain pastures are used for grazing animals.

# Agriculture

Grapes and olives were the most prized crops for trade. Grapes were used to make wine.

Greece had rocky ground and poor soil. It also had nearly 300 days of sunshine and long, warm summers. This meant Greece was a great place to grow olives, grapes, figs, and grains. Barley was the most successful grain because it did not need much water to grow well.

The Greek people ate the crops they grew. They also used them to trade for goods they could not produce at home. Syria, Turkey, and Egypt were a few of the neighboring countries with which the Greeks traded.

This statue from the sixth century BC shows a Greek farmer using oxen to pull a plow.

# Diet in Ancient Greece

Besides the main crops of olives, barley, figs, and grapes, Greeks also grew onions, cabbages, pumpkins, melons, lentils, and garlic. The meadows in the mountains made good grazing land for sheep and goats.

Olive trees prefer poor soil and little rain. That is why they grow so well in Greece's rocky landscape. Greeks used olives in cooking and for their oil.

The people of ancient Greece ate a lot of figs. Like the olive, figs can grow in dry, rocky places.

These animals were mainly raised for their milk. Many ancient Greek families also kept quails and chickens, which were used for their eggs.

Fish was the main source of protein. Meats, such as pork and goat, were eaten in small amounts, too. Historians tell us that the Greeks ate mainly bread, goat cheese, figs, honey, eggs, fish, and water or wine.

# Mining for Metals

Greece's rocky land may not have been easy to grow crops in, but it provided other resources. The ancient Greeks were able to mine for **precious** metals and minerals. The mountains of Thrace and the island of

Greek metal products were valuable trade items. An item like this finely carved gold medallion could have been traded for many useful products.

The Greeks used metals to make weapons and armor, such as this bronze helmet. Bronze was made by mixing together melted copper and tin.

Sifnos were known for their rich supplies of gold and silver. Laurium, near Athens, had silver and iron ore. Cyprus was known for its copper.

These metals were used to make many useful and beautiful items. They could be used for coins, jewelry, armor, weapons, tools, vases, and more.

# Forced to Trade

Some resources, such as limestone and marble, were plentiful throughout Greece. Most resources were not, though. Some city-states might have had all the resources they needed to live, such as good farmland, pastures, and mines.

These were tools used in ancient Greece. If a region did not have access to metal, it might have to trade for tools such as these.

Greek people used their plentiful limestone and marble to carve statues and build temples. Other countries would trade for these raw materials to use in their own buildings.

Most city-states were not that lucky. A city-state might have good farmland, but no access to metals to make tools or weapons. Another city-state might have lots of mines but **barren** land. These places needed to trade with each other for the things they could not produce on their own.

City-states traded with one another. They also traded with neighboring countries.

# The Mediterranean Sea

One of the greatest resources available to the people of ancient Greece was the Mediterranean Sea. It provided a large supply of fish. It also provided a way to reach other places.

Much of ancient Greece was made up of islands. These people needed to sail to neighboring islands and the Greek mainland

This painting on a vase from ancient Greece shows a fisherman with the day's catch.

Ancient Greek ships had masts and sails. Smaller trading ships generally stayed close to the shore. Larger warships had sails and oars. It took around 170 men to row them.

to trade for goods. People on the Greek peninsula also used the sea to travel to neighboring places. Shipbuilding became an important business in ancient Greece due to the closeness of the sea.

# At Port

Many ports were created along the coasts and on the Greek islands. Traders from Syria, Egypt, Turkey, and other neighboring countries visited these ports. Some of the things traded included gold, wool, dyes, and **papyrus**. Thera and Amnisos were two of Greece's prosperous port cities.

This fresco shows the busy port of Thera in ancient Greece. Today this city is commonly called Santorini.

These are ruins from Thera. The settlement there was built on cliffs nearly 1,300 feet (400 m) above the sea.

Many people who lived inland moved to the port cities of Greece. They hoped to become wealthier in these places. It was also more convenient to live where trade was happening. Trips back and forth across the mountains and over land were hard.

# Two City-States

Two of the biggest city-states in ancient Greece were Athens and Sparta. These two city-states show just how much geography can shape the way people live.

Athens was on the coast, and its land was **fertile**. As a center of trade, Athens had a peaceful relationship with its neighbors. Over time Athens grew wealthy.

One of the most famous buildings in Athens is the Parthenon, which sits atop the Acropolis. It is a lasting symbol of Athenian culture.

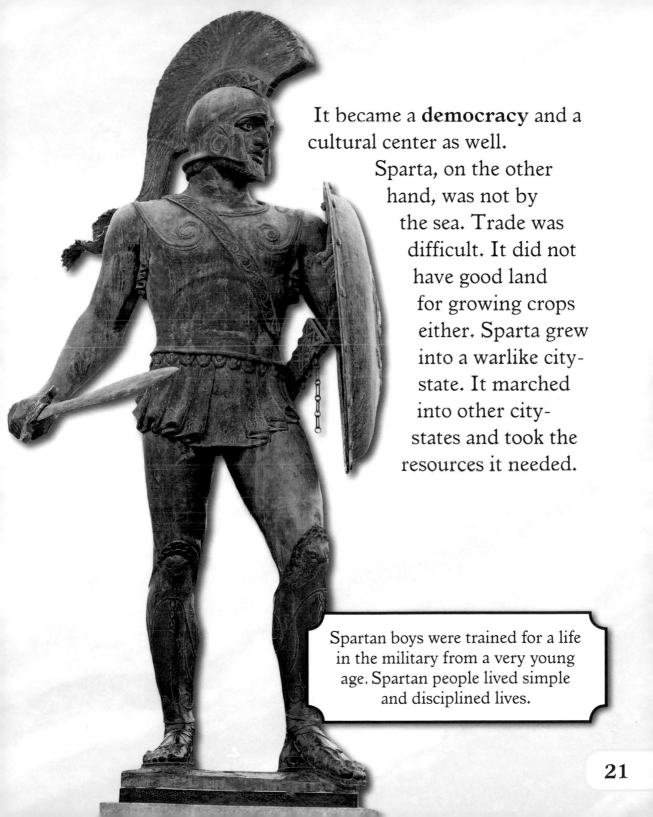

It became a **democracy** and a cultural center as well.

Sparta, on the other hand, was not by the sea. Trade was difficult. It did not have good land for growing crops either. Sparta grew into a warlike city-state. It marched into other city-states and took the resources it needed.

Spartan boys were trained for a life in the military from a very young age. Spartan people lived simple and disciplined lives.

Ancient Greece was a land of farmers, fishers, miners, and merchants. They made use of everything their peninsula and islands had to offer, including the sea. The Greek **civilization** flourished.

Though the people of ancient Greece lived thousands of years ago, their contributions live on. Greece's unique geography shaped its society, and ancient Greek society helped shape our modern world.

The remains of ancient Greece's beautiful art, buildings, and temples remind us of their accomplishments as a civilization.

# GLOSSARY

**barren** (BA-ren) Too poor to produce any crops or vegetation.

**civilization** (sih-vih-lih-ZAY-shun) People living in a certain way.

**climate** (KLY-mit) The kind of weather a certain place has.

**democracy** (dih-MAH-kruh-see) A government that is run by the people who live under it.

**fertile** (FER-tul) Good for making and growing things.

**mineral deposit** (MIN-rul dih-PAH-zut) A place beneath the Earth's surface with a supply of a natural element that is not an animal, a plant, or another living thing.

**natural resources** (NA-chuh-rul REE-sors-ez) Things in nature that can be used by people.

**papyrus** (puh-PY-rus) A type of paper on which ancient peoples wrote, made from the leaves of the papyrus plant.

**pastures** (PAS-churz) Pieces of land where animals eat plants.

**peninsula** (peh-NIN-suh-luh) An area of land surrounded by water on three sides.

**precious** (PREH-shus) Having a high value or price.

# INDEX

# WEBSITES

Due to the changing nature of Internet links, PowerKids Press has developed an online list of websites related to the subject of this book. This site is updated regularly. Please use this link to access the list: www.powerkidslinks.com/sacg/geo/